Draw Quick, Shoot Straight

Back cover photos by: **NANCY LeVine,** www.browneyesgallery.com

Page 6 photo by: **DORI BOCK,** McGinnis Meadows Cattle and Guest Ranch, www.mmgranch.net.

Other books by David Horsey:

From Hanging Chad to Baghdad (2003)

One Man Show (1999)

The Fall of Man (1994)

Cartooning AIDS Around the World (1992)

Horsey's Greatest Hits of the '80s (1989)

Horsey's Rude Awakenings (1981)

Politics and Other Perversions (1974)

Printed and bound in the United States of America.

ISBN 978-0-9800256-0-6

Draw Quick, Shoot Straight

EDITORIAL CARTOONS BY

DAVID HORSEY

Seattle Post-Intelligencer

seattlepi.com

TO MY MOM,
Jeanne Marie Horsey,
the real artist in the family.

When I was four years old, she sat me down with pencils,
crayons and a stack of paper and my career began.

Contents

Introduction

ALL HAT, NO CATTLE

BY DAVID HORSEY

A year ago I spent a week on a ranch in Montana trying to convince a horse to do what I wanted him to do while attempting to make a herd of cattle go where I wanted them to go. This was my first try at fulfilling a lifelong cowboy fantasy.

That fantasy was formed on Saturday mornings when I was a boy sitting in front of a black and white TV watching Roy Rogers and other men with white hats and six guns chasing after bad guys in black hats, all at a full gallop. I was then, and am now, a city boy. Nevertheless, over the years my wardrobe came to include pointy-toed boots, cowboy hats, Wrangler jeans and western shirts with snaps instead of buttons. As this styling choice became a little too obvious to my friends, I perceived I would look a little ridiculous unless I garnered a few skills to match my clothing.

My first serious riding lessons were taken in the wide-open spaces of Los Angeles and, later, on suburban trails outside of Seattle. Eventually, though, I wanted to mount up somewhere in the real West — hence, the stint at the ranch in Montana.

It all went pretty well. I learned to play my role on a team of cowboys holding a couple hundred meandering cattle together as we moved them to new pastures. I took an imperfect but successful shot at cutting cow and calf pairs from the herd. And I rode without saddle sores — and without falling off.

It helped that the horses at the ranch were superbly trained, thus giving me a more positive assessment of my horsemanship than was warranted. I figured that out the following week when I was at Lake Chelan over in Central Washington.

There was a woman at Chelan whom I'd met the previous summer who kept three horses up by the rodeo grounds. She was amenable to letting me go for rides up in the hills and out into the orchards. This time she put me on a gelding that had not been ridden for months, except by a few school kids who mostly got bucked off. Feeling as if I'd earned my chaps at the ranch, I figured I could handle him and I set out on my own.

The horse fought with me right from the start and, in short order, took off at a gallop with no encouragement from me. Actually, I wanted to discourage him, but the cranky horse had tossed his head as he began his run and flipped the reins over to one side of his neck. I couldn't pull back to stop him, I could only pull to the side. This is a little like losing the brakes in a car and having to gear down to make the thing halt. Eventually, my frantic tugging to the left got the job done, but all my overconfidence was scared out of me. This horse was not ready to be ridden by a cowboy-in-training; he needed someone who could show him who was boss. I headed straight back to the corral before anything else happened and spent the next hour getting back to basics with the horse in a confined space.

This aborted joyride taught me a pretty valuable lesson: You can dress like a cowboy and play at being a cowboy, but until you've really done the work and learned all the lessons (and learned that, with horses, you never know it all), you are not a real cowboy.

Which brings me to George W. Bush.

It seems more obvious every day that the Bush kid never realized he got where he was in life because of his daddy. He went to Yale as a legacy and earned a C average. He coasted through his time in the Air National Guard thanks to family connections. His dad's rich buddies bailed him out of his failed career in the oil business and helped him buy into a baseball team. He got credit for doing a few good things as governor of Texas because he let the Democratic Speaker of the House in Austin run the show. And then he became president.

Sadly for us all, he never learned the lesson: You can dress like a president, you can play at being president (you can even be related to a former president), but that doesn't mean you actually know how to be a president.

I cannot think of anyone who more completely fits the derisive description employed by folks out West, "All hat and no cattle." Heck, it's literally the case. He's got his ranch down in Crawford, Texas. He's got his hat and his pickup truck and his drawl and his swagger, but there's not a horse or steer in sight, only those weeds he likes to cut during his extended vacations.

More crucially, he's all hat and no cattle when it comes to governing. Think of Hurricane Katrina and the still languishing city of New Orleans. Think of his plans for Social Security reform and immigration reform that went nowhere. Think of the lip service he gave to being a budget hawk while failing to veto a single pork barrel project passed by the Republican Congress. Think of the justifiable war in Afghanistan that got put on hold while Bush opted to invade Iraq with no coherent plan for what to do with that country after it became an American rebuilding project. Think of the U.S. armed forces on the brink of a breakdown. Think of Osama

9

10

bin Laden still on the loose.

It is the shocking incompetence of the Bush presidency that has made so many people desperate to see the man leave the White House — and I'm talking about conservatives. Republican congressmen no longer want to do business with him. Republican presidential contenders are running from him. And the big thinkers in the conservative think tanks who gave Bush all his ideas in the first place now complain that he has made a mess of their grand designs.

Of course, it is not all the president's fault; he had help.

His vice president, Dick Cheney, his secretary of defense, Donald Rumsfeld, and all those neo-con dreamers, like Paul Wolfowitz, sold him on the idea that American soldiers would be greeted with gift bags and party hats when they rolled into Baghdad.

My job is to sound an alarm when danger is near and, with this crew, there have been so many alarms to sound.

———

Karl Rove, his political guru, succeeded in getting him elected and then re-elected by the slimmest of margins, yet the Rove ethic of making everything about politics infected all aspects of the administration and led to some of the biggest failures. Making political loyalty, rather than competence, the primary qualification for those chosen to run the occupation of Iraq proved utterly disastrous. Injecting partisan politics into the legal decisions of the Justice Department led to

an ongoing scandal. Pandering to preserve the support of social conservatives skewed government policy away from sound science and into the realm of mythology.

Politically, it all worked . . . for a while. But the country will be a long time recovering from the damage done to the environment, to our long-range economic well being, to people's faith in government and to American prestige in the world.

On the plus side, this has all been great for political cartoonists like me. George W. Bush, his no-longer-merry men and his Iraqi quagmire have made it easy to fill my space on the editorial page day after day. Presidents are always leading men in the cast of characters who take the stage in the ongoing morality play of editorial cartoons, but this guy has dominated my work more than most. Why?

Because my job is to sound an alarm when danger is near and, with this crew, there have been so many alarms to sound.

I have become a bit obsessed with finding new ways to say the same thing over and over to readers who continue to think this president is doing just fine. I want to tell them that this is not about conservatives versus liberals or patriots versus cut-and-runners, it is about arrogant incompetence that has put the land I love in increased peril — peril coming not only from new generations of terrorists inflamed by a botched war, but by a fiscal policy that pays for today's excesses with the dollars of our children and an environmental policy that opens the door to calamity for us all.

So far, no one has sent me a message to say, "Gosh, I'm sorry I called you all those nasty names in my last e-mail, you actually are right about this Bush guy." There's nothing new about that. Editorial cartoonists don't change minds; they reinforce people's foregone conclusions. Still, I hope I play some tiny role in nudging the nation away from the precipice.

If nothing else, my cartoons provide a satirical record of the times in which we live, the people who make the news, the events that rattle our world and the newest twists on the age-old theme of human folly. On my desk in my office at the newspaper I display a framed quote from President John F. Kennedy: "There are three things that are real: God, human folly and laughter. The first two are beyond comprehension, so we must do what we can with the third." Employing laughter to help us all cope with the incomprehensible is the task I take on every day and this book, like those I have done before, is my way of reminding myself it is a task worth doing.

I've been drawing editorial cartoons for a long time now and there are many days it feels as if I've done every possible idea three times. Standing alone, many of my cartoons seem trivial exercises in stating the obvious. When I gather the best of them together, though, and deliver them in a coherent sequence, they seem a bit more consequential. They tell a story and make an argument. They are not just jokes; they are journalism.

So, I guess I'll keep doing this cartoon gig for a bit longer — at least until I can handle a horse as well as I can push a pen (and that could take a real long time). Like an Old West gunslinger, I just need to keep my eye on a hundred moving targets while facing down those relentless deadlines. As any cowboy can tell you, the trick to doing that is tough but simple: Draw quick, shoot straight.

— *August 2007*

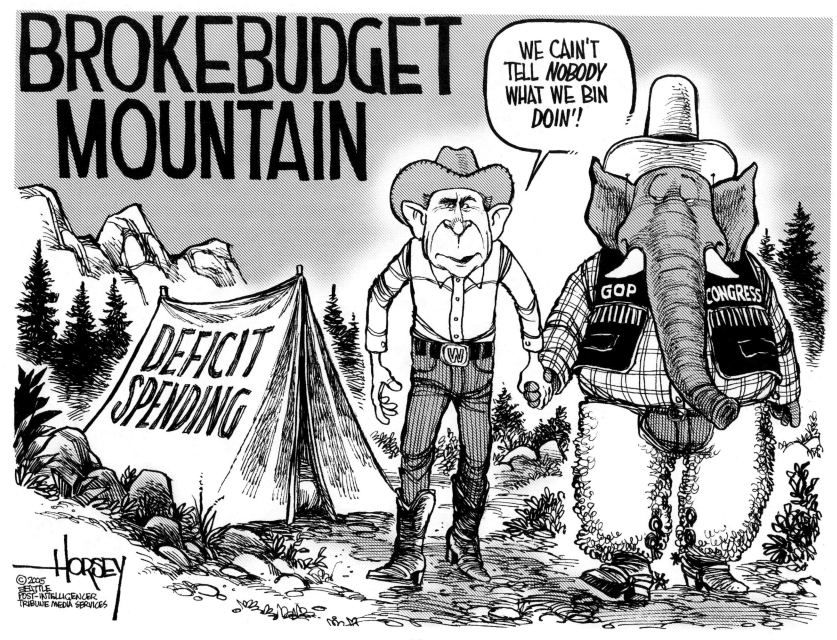

Mr. Bush's Baby

15

16

AN EXPENSIVE BABYSITTER...

20

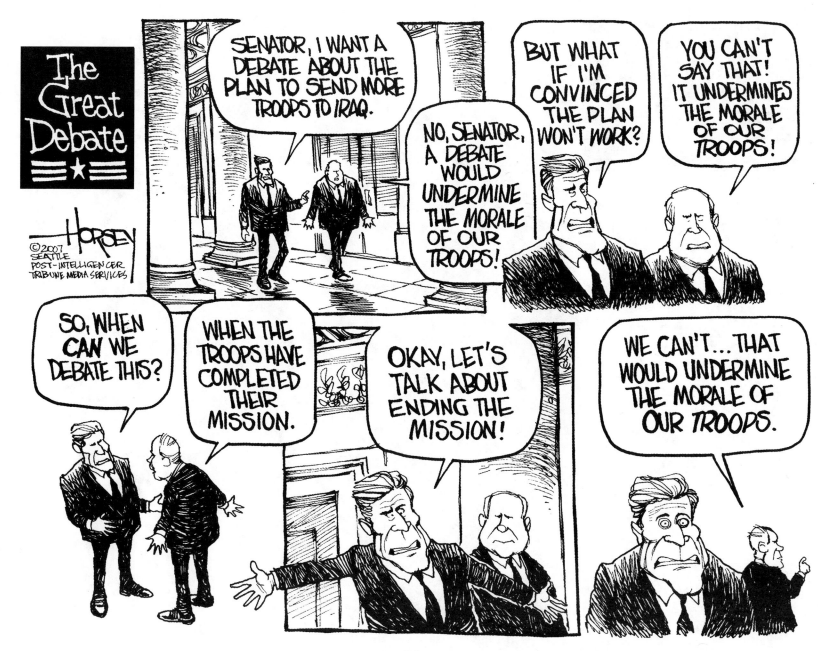

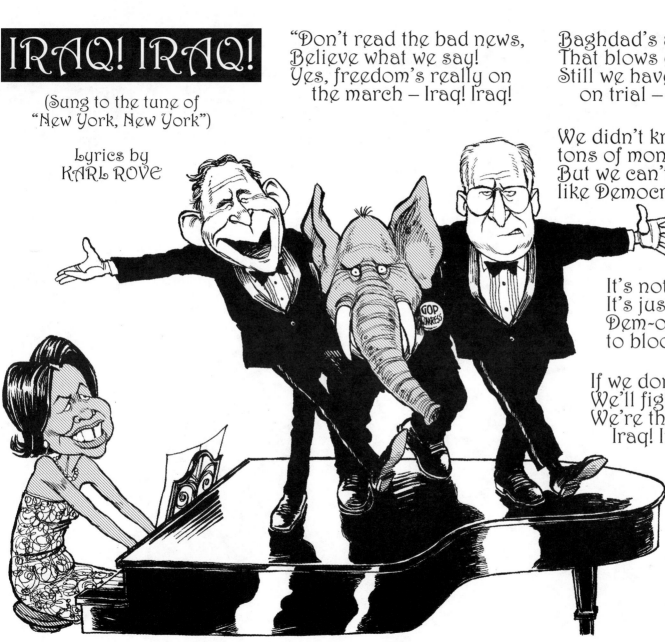

IRAQ! IRAQ!

(Sung to the tune of "New York, New York")

Lyrics by
KARL ROVE

"Don't read the bad news,
Believe what we say!
Yes, freedom's really on
    the march — Iraq! Iraq!

Baghdad's a lit fuse
That blows every day,
Still we have put Saddam
    on trial — Iraq! Iraq!

We didn't know it would cost
tons of money and troops,
But we can't just cut and run
like Democrat dupes!

It's not civil war,
It's just a small spat,
Dem-o-cra-cy is bound
    to bloom in old Iraq!

If we don't fight 'em there
We'll fight 'em over here!
We're there to stay --
    Iraq! Iraq!"

24

26

"OKAY, LET'S SAY IT *ISN'T* A MIRAGE... IT *STILL* LOOKS LIKE A *LONG, LONG WALK!*"

28

· THE BIG JOKE ·

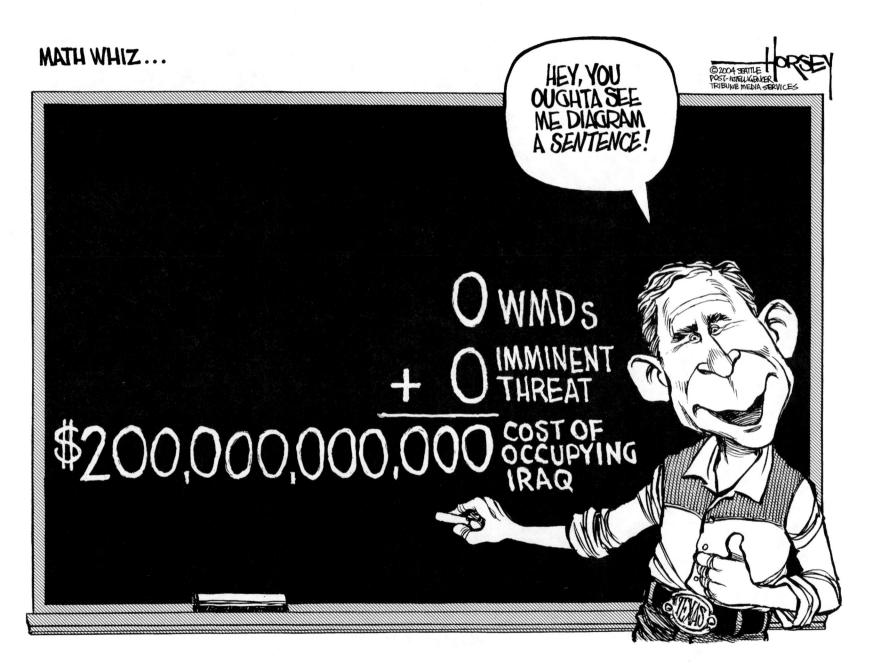

33

34

35

36

38

39

40

41

42

43

44

45

47

48

49

THAT WHICH IS MOST TERRIFYING TO A MILITANT ISLAMIC FUNDAMENTALIST:

A GIRL WITH A SCHOOL BOOK.

51

52

THE MIND OF AL-QAIDA

THE HEART OF AL-QAIDA

THE SOUL OF AL-QAIDA

HORSEY
© 2004
SEATTLE POST-
INTELLIGENCER
TRIBUNE MEDIA
SERVICES

"MY COVER'S BLOWN! THEY'RE CLOSING IN!... NO, NOT AL-QAIDA, IT'S THOSE GUYS FROM THE WHITE HOUSE!"

Empire Rising II

58

59

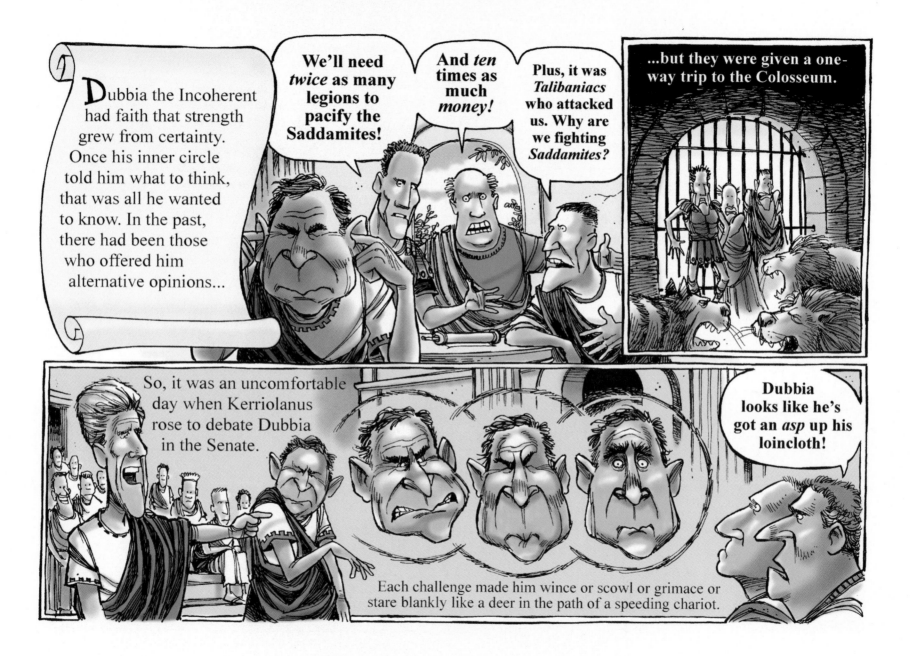

The debate led many to wonder if Kerriolanus had more *gravitas* than the incumbent. Wanting no more confrontations, Dubbia scurried back to the friendly, hand-picked crowds who loved hearing his fanciful version of reality...

Jupiter sends thunderbolts to light the path of our legions. Then, Mars leads them into battle, Apollo melts the swords of the bad guys and we win! *Freedom's on the march!*

ONE EMPIRE UNDER THE GODS

WE ♥ DUBBIA

Meanwhile, Dickchenius Maximus and Rover the Spinner played on people's fears...

If Kerriolanus wins, the Saddamites will murder you in your beds!

And your sons will develop lisps and limp wrists!

The streets of Rome churned with angry partisans as the Senate gathered to vote.

SENATE

"Sic transit gloria mundi." Those words whispered in the ears of victorious Roman generals were a reminder that the glory of the world passes quickly. But no honest voice spoke to Dubbia the Incoherent. Rove the Spinner told Dubbia only what he wanted to hear:

Dubbia, you're doing a *heck* of a job!

But fate always leaves a banana peel to slip on. That moment came for Dubbia when Mount Vesuvius erupted, raining fire on Pompei...

Thousands of poor people fled their homes and huddled in a sports stadium waiting for food, water and rescue.

Dubbia's power began to rapidly erode. One by one, his trusted advisers fell out of favor and were tossed to the lions -- Rummi, master of the legions, Wolfowitz the Scribe, Gonzalius of Hispania, Rove the Spinner and Scooterius the Fibber...

PRESS BOX

Yes! Let them eat **Scooterius** while we sneak **out** of here!

Dickchenius Maximus, the vice-consul, shot a friend while hunting in Sicily...

It's not *my* fault you look like a deer!

W-w-why did you shoot me?!

Made a laughingstock, he retreated to an undisclosed catacomb to hatch new schemes in the darkness.

War in *Persia!* *That's* the ticket!

JUDEA

MESOPOTAMIA

PERSIA

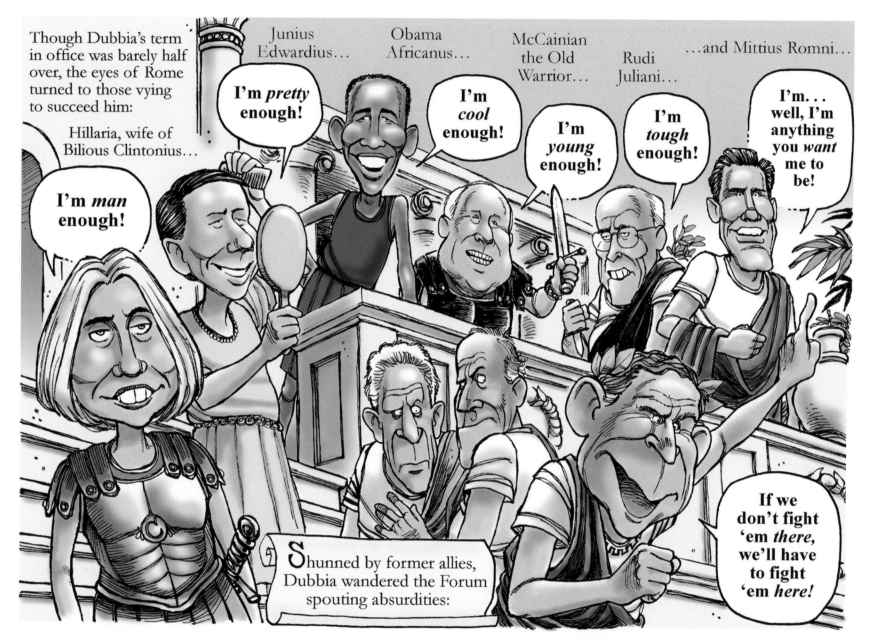

71

The Permanent Campaign

73

HIS
CHRONIC
DEPRESSION
WAS NEVER
PROPERLY
TREATED.

A FAILURE
IN BUSINESS,
HE GOT RICH
AS AN
OPPORTUNISTIC
TRIAL
LAWYER.

HIS ONLY
POLITICAL
EXPERIENCE
WAS ONE
SOLITARY
TERM IN
CONGRESS.

WHILE OUR
TROOPS WERE
FIGHTING TO
LIBERATE
CALIFORNIA,
HE OPPOSED
THE WAR.

IF HE'D BEEN
IN CHARGE,
LOS ANGELES,
PHOENIX AND
SAN FRANCISCO
WOULD BELONG
TO MEXICO.

IS THIS THE MAN WE WANT
AS COMMANDER IN CHIEF?

PAID FOR BY MEXICAN WAR
VETERANS FOR TRUTH

© 2004
SEATTLE
POST-INTELLIGENCER
TRIBUNE MEDIA SERVICES

78

80

82

83

89

91

We the People of the United States, in Order to form a more perfect Union, establish Justice, insure domestic Tranquility, provide for the common defence, promote the general Welfare, and secure the Blessings of Liberty to ourselves and our Posterity, do ordain and establish this Constitution for the United States of America.
Article I
Article II.
Article III.
Article IV.
DOMESTIC SPYING
CHENEY
OOPS.
HORSEY
©2006 SEATTLE POST-INTELLIGENCER TRIBUNE MEDIA SERVICES

94

95

· SOPRANO FAMILY VALUES ·

"...AND, AS WE LEAD AMERICA IN YOUR RIGHTEOUS PATH, BLESS OUR DEVOUT COLLEAGUES WHO COULD NOT BE WITH US TODAY BECAUSE THEY ARE BEING *INVESTIGATED, INDICTED OR INCARCERATED.*"

100

101

102

103

105

106

110

111

115

116

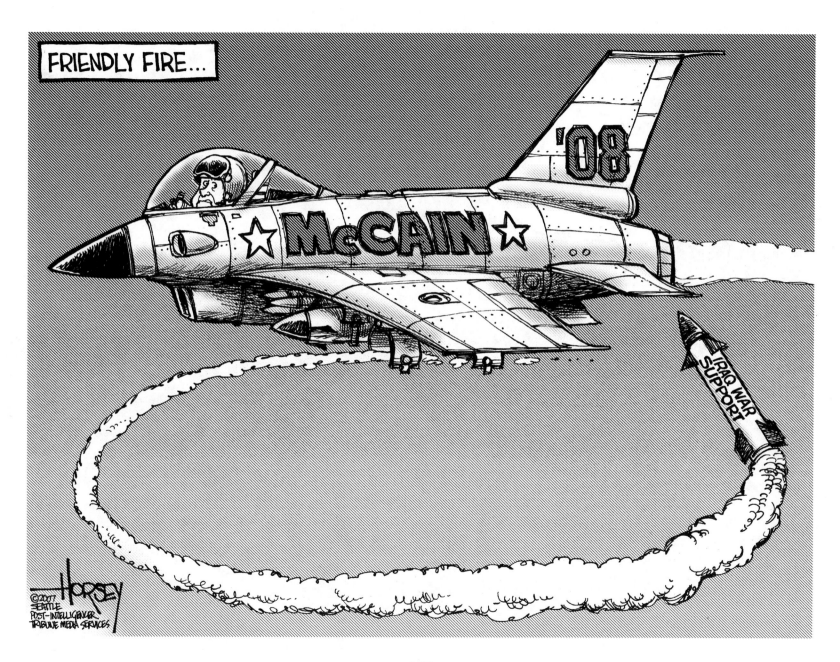

119

Homeland Insecurity

121

122

123

129

133

"MUMMY! DADDY'S NOT GOING TO GIVE AWAY MY *INHERITANCE* TO THE *GATES FOUNDATION*, *IS HE?!*"

HALF OF THE WORLD'S PEOPLE LIVE ON LESS THAN $2 A DAY...

...AND WE WONDER WHY THE WORLD HAS PROBLEMS?

· A NEW WORLD TO CONQUER ·

THE CONSUMER SOCIETY...

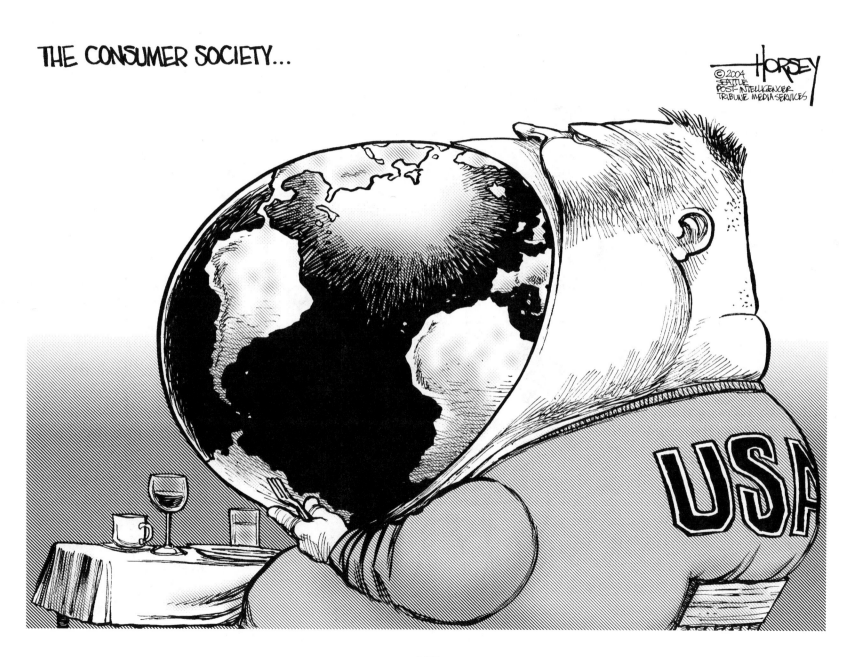

A Climate Carol

(Sung to the tune of "Santa Claus is Coming to Town")

You'd better watch out,
you'll freeze or you'll fry.
That bad green house gas
is filling the sky.
Climate change is
coming to Earth!

Our economy's built
on old fossil fuels.
We think we'll get rich
but really we're fools.
Climate change is
coming to Earth!

The polar caps are melting.
The seas are on the rise.
The glaciers out in Glacier Park
disappear before our eyes!

It's prob'ly too late
to clean up our act.
We just wouldn't sign
the Kyoto pact.
Climate change is
coming to Earth!

Where Santa has his workshop
way up at the North Pole,
they'll soon be planting
palm trees 'cause
we're burning too
much coal!

The storms will get huge.
The coastlines will sink.
The farms will dry up.
We're all on the brink.
Climate change is coming,
climate change is coming,
climate change is
comiiinnnggg
tooo Earrrth!

138

142

"IT HAS COME TO OUR ATTENTION THAT *SOME OF YOU* ARE STILL USING THE SALUTATION *HAPPY NEW YEAR...*"

"THAT PHRASE IS CULTURALLY *INSENSITIVE* TOWARD THOSE WHO USE THE HEBREW, ISLAMIC OR CHINESE CALENDARS..."

"AFTER ALL, THE SO-CALLED *NEW YEAR* IS CALCULATED FROM THE ALLEGED BIRTHDATE OF *YOU-KNOW-WHO...*"

"*THUS, HAPPY NEW YEAR HAS OBVIOUS RELIGIOUS CONNOTATIONS AND SHOULD BE AVOIDED...*"

"WE SUGGEST DISPENSING WITH ANY *YEAR* REFERENCE IN FAVOR OF SOMETHING *NEUTRAL*, LIKE *HAVE A NICE DAY...*"

"EITHER *THAT* OR JUST QUIT *TALKING* TO *STRANGERS!*"

HORSEY

©2006
SEATTLE
POST-INTELLIGENCER
TRIBUNE MEDIA SERVICES

"CONGRATULATIONS! YOU ARE THE 300 MILLIONTH AMERICAN!"

145

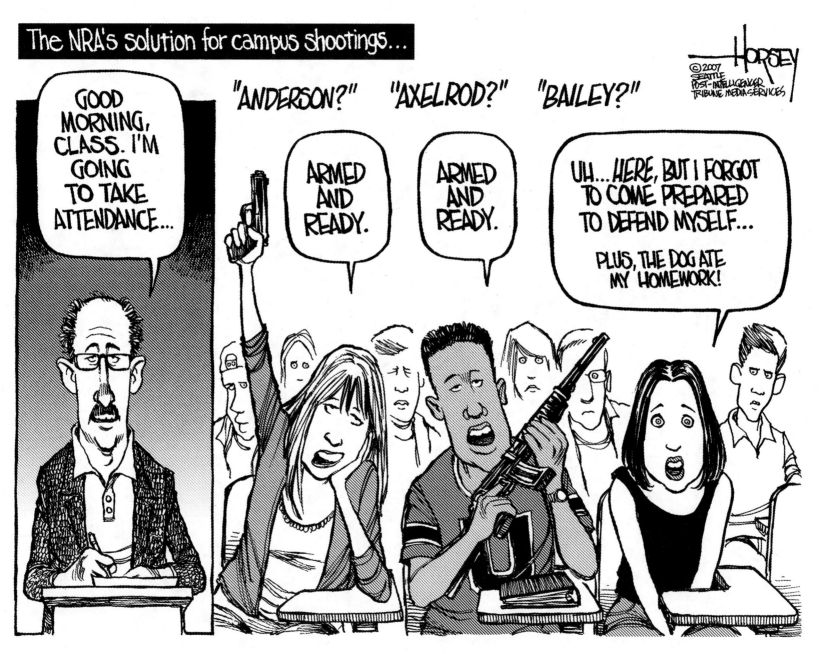

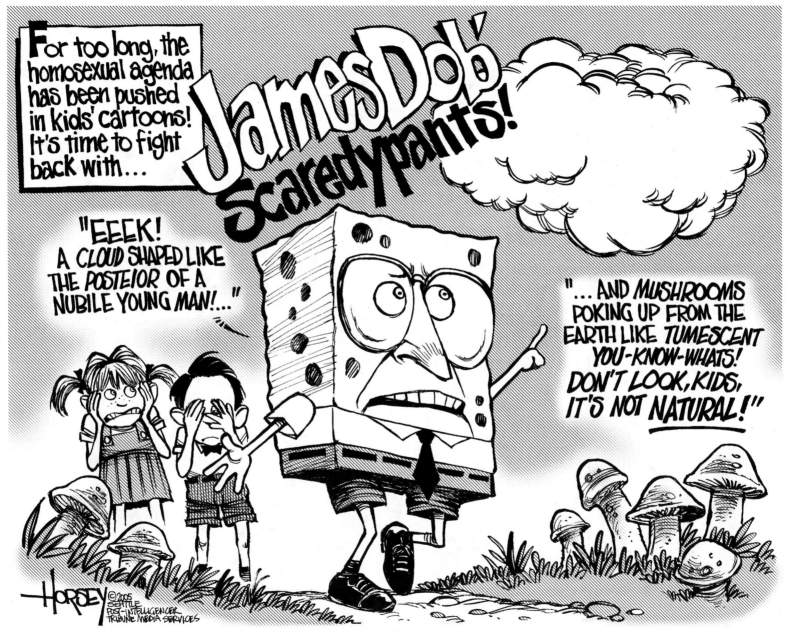

150

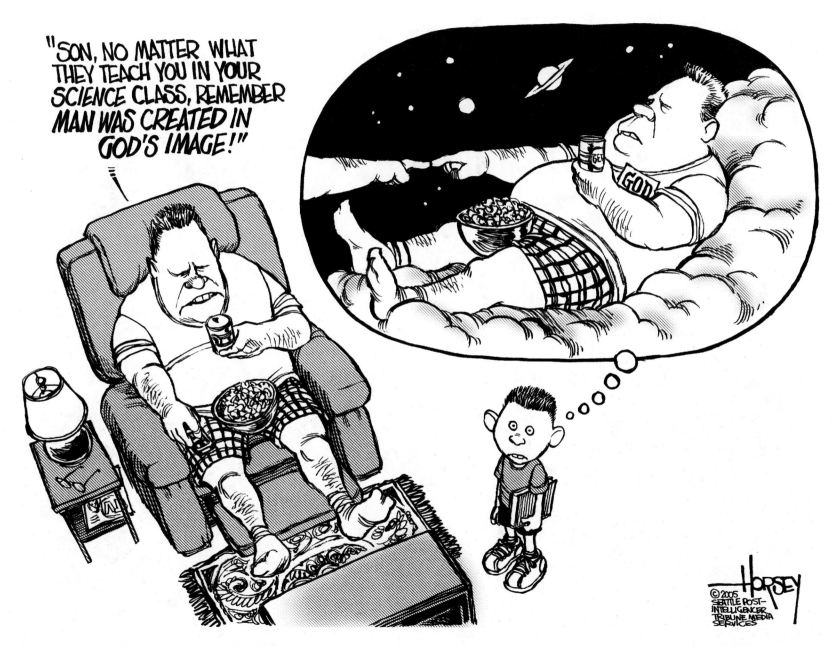

152

153

· WHERE AMERICA STANDS ·

157

Modern life...

Middle America adjusts to the new world revealed at the Super Bowl...

"SO, WHAT WOULD YOU THINK IF I GOT A PAIR OF THOSE *JANET JACKSON* THINGIES?"

161

Rain City Review

165

HOW THE WORLD WORKS: PEOPLE WITH THE LEAST CHANCE OF *KNOWING* HOMOSEXUALS ARE THE MOST LIKELY TO *FEAR* THEM.

167

169

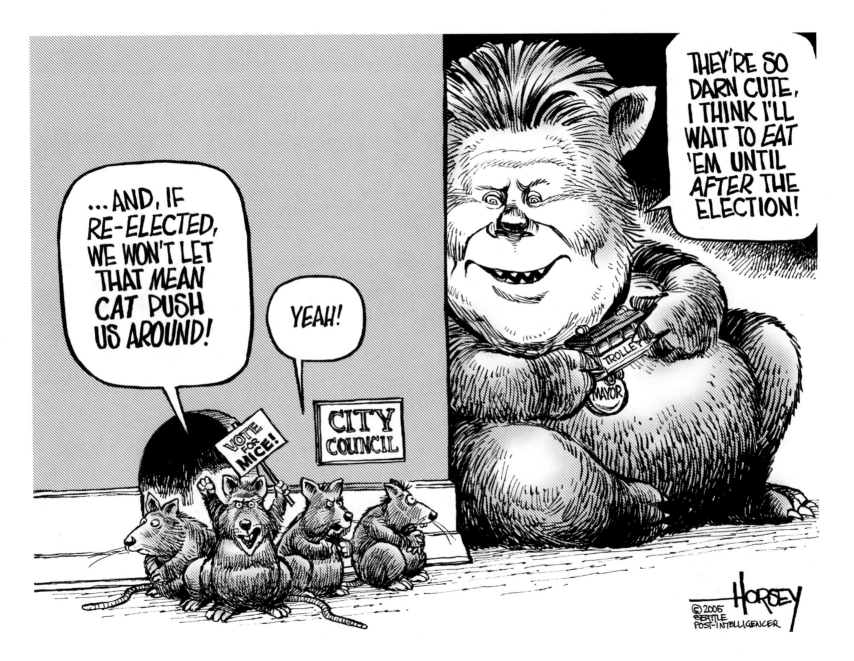

174

When **DAVID HORSEY** was a little boy, it was a close call as to whether he would be a cartoonist or a cowboy. Growing up in Seattle, though, he found cowboy role models scarce while cartooning opportunities kept opening up. So, after nearly three decades at the Seattle P-I, two Pulitzers and one honorary doctorate, it appears cartooning has won out. Still, you never know . . .

About the Author